# easier done than than said

Volume 1
...in case I decide to write more

*by Louise Mita*
*©2021*

Published by:
**The Art Of Energy, Inc.**
Honolulu, Hawaii
www.taoenergy.com

First publication 2021

Library of Congress Registration Number: TXu-2-280-725
ISBN: 979-8-9857096-1-2

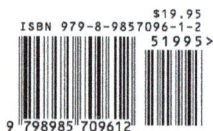

$19.95
ISBN 979-8-9857096-1-2

51995>

9 798985 709612

**Easier Done Than Said**
Written by Louise Mita
Photographs by Luika
Illustrations by Luika

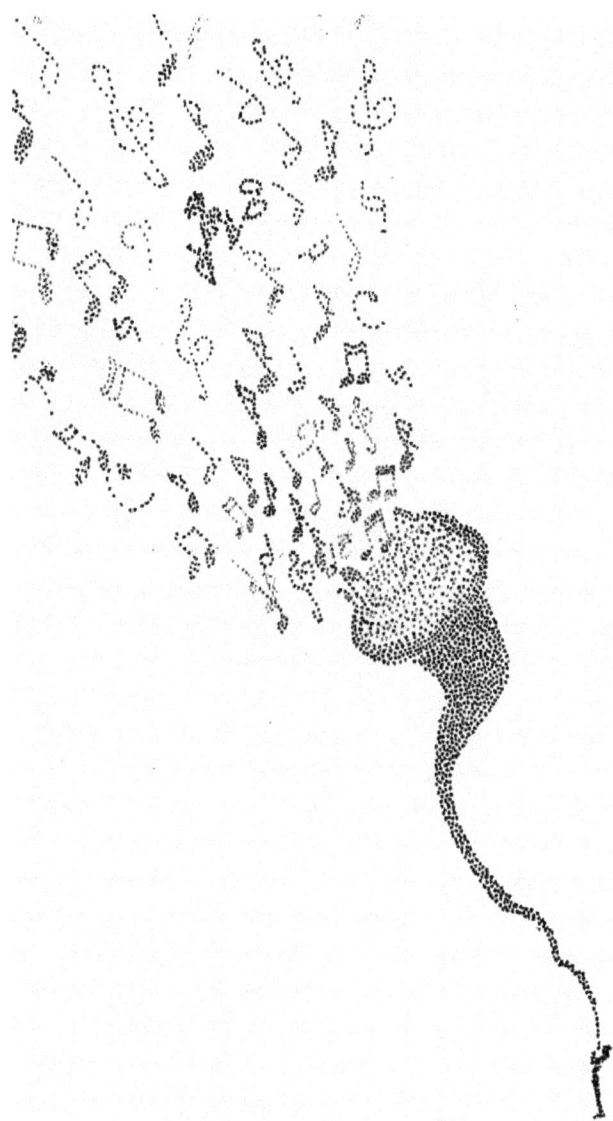

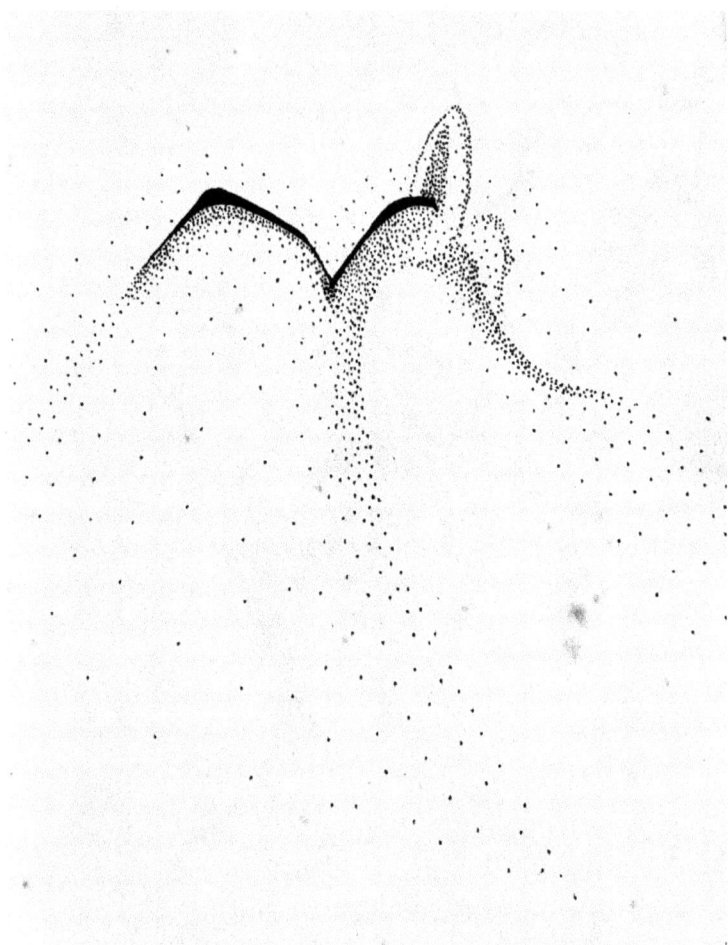

This is dedicated to
mine...
Randy and Nicole

and
Michelle and Dylan
(you're mine too)

and to theirs...
(IOA)
Joey, Castanza, Lycan, Ha'ani,
Shekinah & Nikko


\*\*\*\*\*\*\*


And to YOU
Because you KNOW
You Always KNEW

Destiny is written...

But it's written in pencil...

...Moi

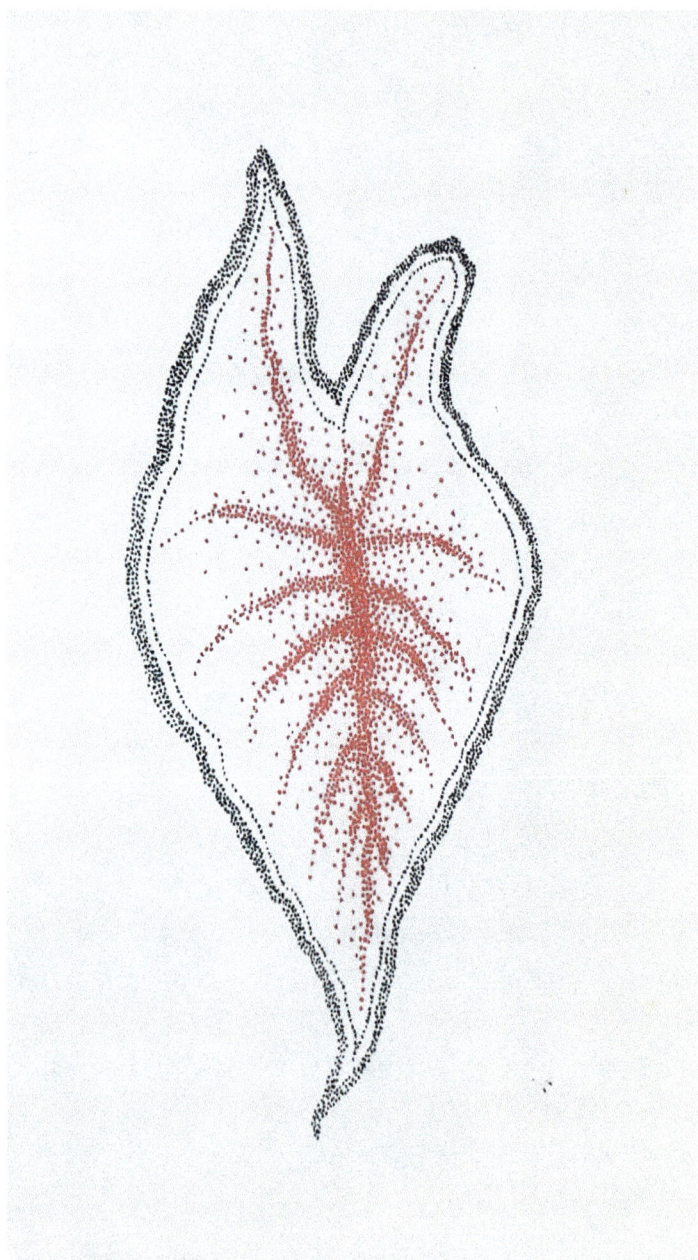

CONTENTS

INTRODUCTION

1. OTOSAN

2. THE MITA IMMIGRATION

3. ROSIE'S GUN

4. 318 LUNCH

5. NEW JERSEY

6. LIKE MOTHER

7. THE PICTURE BRIDE

8. MANNY

9. THE CHARADE

10. SYLVESTER

11. LULU

12. THE MORNING AFTER

13. GERALDINE

14. REVOLUTION

15. C'EST MOI

16. HUNTER

17. LEMONADE STAND

18. SILENT THOUGHTS FOSTER UNDERSTANDING

19. Y'KNOW

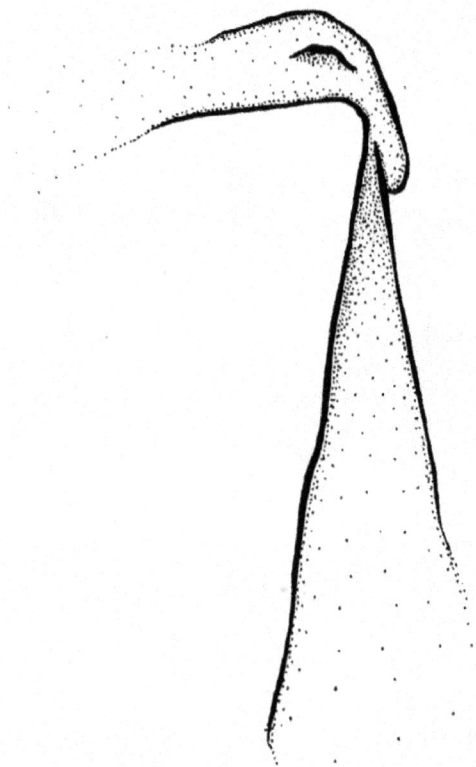

## INTRODUCTION

As our journey continues, seeking knowledge, wisdom, peace of mind; we're basically, trying to figure out what we're doing here on the planet. In the process, we ironically find that we end up where we started; full circle, as they say.

What if we were awake from the beginning? Would we find the path an easier course? Less fraught with stress? Sans fear? More joyous? Comfortable? Peaceful?

Or would it be any different at all?

What if God walked up to you and said, "You're exactly where you are supposed to be and doing everything as planned." Would you feel better about yourself? Would that be enough to make you appreciate all that you have and don't have; perhaps even rendering you happy?

We're so much alike: and we're all on that quest – doing what we do and hoping we're on the right path, or at least going in the right direction.

A vertical upward ascent...


MEET ME AT THE PEAK...

OTOSAN:  YOSABURO MICHISHITA

# 1. OTOSAN

It was cold and wet; my feet were numbed. Shadows in the trees were staring at us; things looked bigger than they were because of the darkness of the forest. Weaving through hanging nooses filled me with anxiety. So many sounds startling me every step of the way - I just wanted to get out - go home. I was on the verge of panic for about three hours. Then it happened...

In the distance, we saw it moving - slowly but very sure of itself as it stared directly at us. Our breathing ceased; we froze. I tried to retract my eyes so he wouldn't see me see him - but he did and he started toward us. No time. No thought. I couldn't hear for the pounding of my heart. I couldn't hold my breath any longer.

I started panting and gasping as we began running backward - never leaving him out of our vision. He moved swiftly through the shadows as branches creaked and vines swung hitting me - hitting us - hitting him. He was gaining ground rapidly.

Then Otosan stopped and drew his arrow from his back and lodged it into the bow in one motion. Drew, aimed and released within a fraction of a second that lasted forever. We watched the arrow glide to its target in slow motion. Silence. Stillness all around except for the whirrrr of the arrow. And it hit - bull's eye.

The forest whispered and began to come to life as we exhaled - almost completely. We were frozen for what felt like hours waiting for a sound, a movement, a cry, a drop. The arrow struck its target. No doubt.

The chase was over - we knew the panic of being the prey - but we won – we had survived.

It was...a TIGER! An actual tiger in Japan. We had never seen or heard of one, ever, in our small village in the countryside of our land. We both knew he would have eaten us - killed us miserably and eaten us so Otosan reacted with warrior speed to save our lives.

I was drenched. As I began to thaw out I walked carefully behind my father, watching him slowly approach the tiger anticipating instant revival. He kept his second arrow in his bow - slightly taut - just in case. He nodded at me to stay behind and to the side as we approached, not once taking his eyes off the tiger.

The dense jungle forest made it difficult to determine if it was still breathing as the pulse of every quivering leaf caste waves of movement and currents of energy all around. For a moment, he lost sight of its position as a gust of wind blew across our path. The sun shimmering through the tall trees shifted the dimensions of our world and we froze until things settled again.

It felt like an eternity and miles of slow motion walking - creeping until we could see the arrow standing tall in its victim. Huge - motionless. Shadowed in leaves and branches where he had fallen - no sign of life at all.

Otosan lowered his bow and approached the last 20 feet with curiosity more than fear. I kept my distance as his instruction hadn't changed. But then he stopped - and froze once again - with a stillness that shattered the anticipation of our approach. I stopped and waited...waited...waited until I couldn't stand the suspense. Then I slowly trotted toward him - the last fifteen feet accelerating as he never turned to acknowledge my presence. And then I saw it. Stunned like Otosan - we stood there for hours staring…staring at the arrow imbedded deeply into a boulder.

And that was the beginning of my journey into the world I live in now. My father's account of a story told by his father, as a young boy hunting with his Otosan in Japan.

I was riveted - as much as that arrow in the boulder. I didn't know why but I felt moved, inspired, driven to do just that - shoot an arrow into a stone; penetrate the impenetrable. Walk through walls. It seemed relatively simple. I knew I could do it. Actually, I didn't know there was anything I couldn't do. I even knew I could fly - I felt it so clearly in my dreams and I knew that being awake I could only refine the technique with practice.
I knew anything was possible.

*Naoto Michishita: age 15 passport photo 1920*

## 2. The Mita Immigration

My Dad and Uncle Buddy came to America when they were 15 and 13, respectively. Their father, my grandfather, Yosaburo Michishita, brought them to Kentucky where he worked for the railroad as a cook - and got them jobs doing manual labor of any kind just so they could be in America. This was the promise land; a place of opportunity and possibility that was impossible in Japan.

My grandfather got a job working on a boat that took over a month at sea to reach its destination; America. When it finally docked he climbed into a box and threw himself overboard with the intention of fleeing Japan to start a new life in America. If the lid hadn't opened he could have floated away and none would have been the wiser. But as fate would have it the box overturned and he was discovered swimming downstream toward his freedom. They caught the runaway and he was punished and returned to Japan.

The next voyage, working on another boat headed to America served him better as his experience made him wiser. This time he did the same escape but when his box overturned and he spilled out, he swam against the current to the river mouth - then upstream in that river. He managed to avoid capture, stay alive, and somehow, made his way to Kentucky. It wasn't his intended destination. He didn't know there was a Kentucky. He was a man of immediate actions and no long thought out plans. Let's get to step one and we'll figure it out from there. Clearly this came from his childhood training, observing his father shooting arrows into boulders. Within a year he figured his way to Kentucky.

When he was finally able to secure permanent employment in America he had to give up a lot of what he knew and adopt a whole new world. He got a job working as a cook for the railroad the Chinese were building. The first thing he had to give up was his name. It was too long. They were used to the sound of one syllable Chinese names. The American boss decided "Mi-chi-shi-ta" was a waste of ink and annunciation so they cut out the middle two syllables and he would now be known as Mita.

His mission was to establish himself well enough in America so that he could go back to Japan, retrieve his two sons and return with them to the land of opportunity. Which he did. All the details of that were not as harrowing as his first or second voyage as they immigrated with passports and photos and their soon to be Japanese-American last name, Mita.

My grandfather had accomplished what he intended and the mission was over. This was the noblest deed a good father could do to provide the best opportunities for his sons. Now he was more than eager to return to the motherland.

Shortly after their arrival, when the boys were settled in, with very little notice, my grandfather left America and went back to Japan for good.

So, there was my father - 15 years old - along with his little brother of 13, neither speaking English or knowing anything about this new country, culture, or life at all, for that mattter. All they knew was that their father said this would be better than what they had in Japan and this was what they would have now. Be strong. Be smart. Good luck. Sayonara.

Yoshio Michishita: age 13;  Naoto Michshita: age 15

## 3. ROSIE'S GUN

 My mother would walk outside with me and we would look up at the noisy flying car that she called "an arrow-plane" and said my father was on it. Every day. And she'd tell me to wave at it. Every day. We were living in Hawaii with my grandparents in the house my mother grew up in. I don't remember how we got there from the Bronx but this wasn't home. I could tell there was something foreign and strange about it but as a 2-year-old, 'strange' is normal because everything is new. Even so, it did feel... strange. And there was something amiss about waving at that noisy flying car that my dad was on – every day. But I went with it. Knowing... it was some sort of a game. For some reason, I could feel an untruth, a pretend, a fake, a make believe. It wasn't disturbing. I wasn't afraid. It just felt ... off. I felt like the RCA dog. But I didn't know the RCA dog at the time. I just went with the program...and waved.

There was a girl on the other side of the wooden fence that I would see every day as we were waving to my Dad. Rosie. My mom would say, "Wave at Rosie." And I would and she would wave back. Unlike my dad. But there was no connection - just a wave and absolutely no feeling of "I want to play with you, I recognize you, I'm happy to see you again today, you're becoming a familiar fixture on the other side of the fence"...nothing.

Then one day I walked up to the fence and we stared at each other. She showed me her blue plastic gun which to me was a blue thing - and I stuck my hand through the fence to touch it - her blue thing - and she bit my finger.

21

The world stopped. I tried to retract my hand as the pain kicked in and I screamed. My mother came to the rescue and all I knew was I would never wave at that girl again. I stopped crying. I wasn't afraid or alarmed - I was mad. I clearly remember that feeling. And I never smiled at her again. With all my mother's coaxing - I was mad when I saw her. Every day. So, I stopped looking at her. Because I didn't want to be mad. Or did I? Or was I? But what I realized was that I was mad at myself. I knew it was my fault for sticking my arm through a fence and getting bitten. It was my fault - not hers. I owned it. I was 2.

No one actually witnessed the incident as it happened. No one could tell me about it. Rosie was probably 3. We didn't have words. Reasoning. Analysis. Conversation. Reprimand. Nothing. But we had a knowing. I had a knowing. And a lesson of sorts that transformed me at that moment...forever. And I remember it to this day with the visceral awareness of being right there. That feeling of being mad...at myself.

There were 2Me's. One that looked through my eyes and saw it happen; felt it; smelled it; on the ground level looking straight across...was "In It". And the Other Me that watched from the outside - the witness; observer. Who felt nothing. Didn't have an opinion. Like a camera recording it all. Saving the imagery and revisiting it later as often as necessary or desired.

Most of my significant moments have been experienced by the 2Me's. Interesting to note, "tumi," not the luggage brand, is the Bangla word for "you," and Zulu for "happy." Feel that tingle in your tummy below your naval? That is your place of KNOWING. That place in you that is YOU. It says, "aahhhaaaa..." requiring no explanation. I know that's the real

YOU; the real ME. And I'm happy we have a place of knowing.

How do we know? When we are children we know; we just do. The chatter is not there to create debate. We don't have vocabulary. We haven't learned to doubt. We are untrained in the skills of rumination, mulling over rationale. We just know. Then we are carefully trained to ignore this knowing and dive into the complexity of contemplation; becoming sensible, logical, thoughtful, analytical, cautious, seeing all sides until we can successfully drown in the confusion of epistemology. And we spend our entire lives trying to get back to the purity - the brilliance - of that knowing.

I knew the waving at the flying car was bull. It felt silly. At 2. I didn't buy it. So, it made me question this woman who makes me do fake stuff. And I appease her. With sincere patronizing intentions. We had an agreement from 2. There were times the 2Me's would stand in unison observing - wondering - shrugging our shoulders before we knew that was a thing - an expression in the physical of what we felt on the inner. Ok. "Whatever." As I got older I discovered that "Whatever" expressed a universal feeling. That was how I made things ok. It still didn't make sense but, "Whatever." The 2Me's agreed to it. To pretend everything was OK…we could just say "Whatever…"

(It's like seeing your boss' fly is open but nobody's going to tell him so we all keep our eyes fixated on his eyes and think, "Whatever".)

Exhibit A: the blue gun

23

24

## 4. 318 LUNCH

There is no understanding of excess or lack as a child. Things are what they are. We are hungry. Or not. Cold or warm. Things are as they seem until someone tells you otherwise. "We're struggling." "Times are hard." "It's so dangerous here." "I'm sorry you can't have whatever you want." Whatever.

None of that had any meaning to me. I was a kid. I lived from the 'In It Me" perspective and life was a gerund: eating, sleeping, playing, laughing, crying, (rarely), doing, doing, doing. Just normal gerunding...as most of us kids do.

My daddy worked in a restaurant on 125th Street and Lenox Avenue in the heart of Harlem, NYC. His main job was working behind the counter "slinging hash," as he would say. He was a short order cook like the ones today behind the scenes in the kitchen at diners like Denny's and Ihop. But the short order cooks of yore were doing it all within a space of 2 body widths from the counter where the customers were seated. The atmosphere was thick with barking orders, lively conversation, sounds of sizzle and clattering dishes, steam, smoke and scrumptious smells. No one handed them a written order; instead, each order was hollered out and had to be remembered, created, plated and handed back while the second and third order was being announced with urgency and specificity as if it were the only one. And my daddy got every order right.

This was absolute heaven to a 3-year-old seeing it for the first time when my daddy brought me with him to visit the restaurant. It was his day off and we went as civilians; it felt so special!

Above the entrance prominently seen from as far as a block away: "318 Lunch" - a big red sign with bold white letters painted by my father. He was very proud of that and I felt proud that he was proud! That was his alter self; the artist. His commercial money making artistic self was a "Show card artist." Show card artists were not considered sign painters but writers whose flare for calligraphy and stylized lettering would render hand painted signs in businesses or restaurants like this. Some signs, like "318 Lunch", or "EXIT" or "Toilet" were permanent and could be admired for months, maybe years. Others were quickies announcing something short-lived but with style and panache if you cared about your business at all. Show card artists provided a need invaluable yet ephemeral. These signs would advertise the menu, the special of the day, featured items for sale, holiday treats and other announcements, many of which had a time limit, thus the same short lifespan for the sign.

The minute we walked in I saw my daddy's signs were everywhere in the restaurant! Even though I couldn't read I could recognize his writing style. On the main wall behind the counter was the menu; on two of the doors were the bathroom signs; there were other signs that looked important because they stood alone; some with colorful numbers; all painted by my daddy.

We walked into a barrage of booming warm friendly greetings. "Hey Mita! Who is the lovely lady?" I met all his friends who were happy and loud and laughing and offered me pie and cocoa as I sat at the counter on a stool that would keep spinning if I didn't have both arms outstretched, hands gripping the counter and my daddy's knee wedged against it. This was a very exciting outing as my mother wasn't with us; something felt daring, wild

26

and just plain fun! I felt so happy to be part of the universe my father escaped to everyday. My world suddenly blew open and doubled in size and possibility! I felt like I shared a secret with my father that my mother didn't know.

I don't remember leaving the restaurant or falling asleep on the bus ride home. I do remember waking up the next day feeling excited and ready to go to work with my daddy from now on.

Somehow my mother didn't share my enthusiasm nor my new career choice as I remained with her every day...and interestingly or not, I can't recall any particulars of that existence.

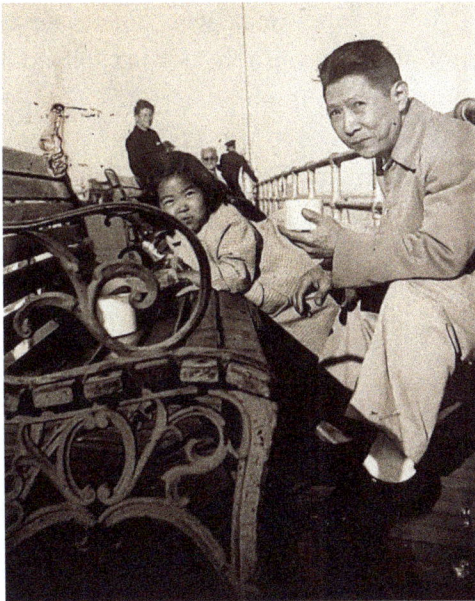

Don't get me wrong; I liked her - but I felt a special connection with my daddy. It seemed like we were the team and she was our mom. We took good care of her because she took good care of us.

I do recall one day when I absolutely HAD to talk to my daddy but he was at work. I desperately NEEDED to. I don't recall if I cried or screamed or what unforgivable behavior I executed but I was relentless and insistent to the point where my mother was driven to do the unfathomable. She called my father ... at work.

In the 1950's this was unheard of. My father wasn't the owner. He wasn't the boss. He wasn't the manager. He was a short order cook. And painted signs. (He was the only one who regarded himself as a show card artist. He was regarded as a sign painter.) And a handy man who did whatever odd jobs were required of him. Because that's what folks did - whatever was necessary to keep your job.

But in the end, my mother called my father at work.

She waited for a small eternity clutching the big black handset and shooting daggers at me every few seconds. Unimpressed I waited - standing close enough without being too close.

Finally, she spoke into the big black handset and said - "Hello, I'm sorry, I'm Mrs. Mita. Mr. Mita's wife. I'm so sorry. May I speak to him please?"

"Hold on Mrs. Mita. I'll send someone to go fetch your husband. He's in the basement working on the boiler." The voice on the phone knew it must have been urgent for a wife to disturb a husband while he was working - especially a man of his position.

28

She nodded her head, bowing and said "Thank you. I'm sorry. Thank you," as if they could see her obsequious bow repeated three, four, five times.

Then she was silent for a loooong time. She stared upward at the ceiling, blinking. I stared too, wondering what she was looking at. She didn't even take the time to glare at me as she was so absorbed.

"Hello? Hello? I'm so sorry...blahblahblah Louise wants to talk to you. Yes. I know. I'm sorry. She blahblahblah" and handed me the phone with a look of shame and disgust - a look I was very familiar with.

"Hi Daddy! Hi! I just wanted to say Hi! I miss you! What are you doing?"

He said "blahblahblahblah give your mother the phone."

I did and walked away, satisfied, back to my unmemorable playing or whatever I did. They spoke for another brief moment. I heard my mother repeat "I'm sorry" a few times between the "blahblahblahs."

When he finally came home that evening, seemingly later than his usual 4am to 7pm day, he was quiet; serious; somber (my grown up today interpretation). He walked in slowly and looked at my mother then me then her then me. He came up to me and picked me up and hugged me. Slow and tight. And held on for a little longer than usual.

It felt normal. No big deal. It felt normally nice - hugs from my daddy always felt nice. Then as he put me down he told my mother "blahblahblah - *he was working on the broken boiler in the basement with his friend that morning. After the phone call, he took a break and sat down at the counter and had a cup of coffee before going back downstairs - then suddenly... BOOM!!! The boiler exploded... no... no... blahblahblah... my friend... no... ambulance... no... blahblahblah*".

Then he turned and came back to me and knelt down to my height and said, "You saved my life." and picked me up and hugged me again. "Uh huh." I hugged him back and went back to gerunding after he put me down.

That was that. No thing. No feeling. No understanding at all what he meant by the "saved my life" comment. That meant nothing at all to me.

Nor why I HAD to speak to him.

Nor why my mother conceded to my rant.

No idea what that day was about... no idea at all.

I thought to myself, "blahblahblah..."

## 5. NEW JERSEY

What I loved most about my dad were the cool stories he would tell about facing struggles and overcoming the odds every time. He told me that on more than one occasion he had nothing to eat and was so hungry he walked into a restaurant and ask if he could wash dishes or do anything for a meal. It sounded resourceful to me and I thought of it as a clever way to survive and carry on with his adventures. I think these stories were meant to highlight what a great life we're living now and that we should appreciate how fortunate we are.

We were the modern American family with tales of old sounding like fantasies and bedtime stories. But anytime he'd talk about his brother, Uncle Buddy, it was special. And KayKay, Uncle Buddy's only daughter, seemed more important than I could understand. She was my only relative on my father's side - my cousin - my dad's niece - and my nemesis. She was a year and three months older than I and the one person I was constantly compared to and designated as my role model. It brought out the Rosie's gun feeling in me.

Anytime we went to visit them was a special occasion. Coming from the projects in Harlem to their house in New Jersey was an excursion on a train, then a bus then someone picking us up at the bus depot then driving in a car to her house. So, it only happened once or twice a year. We lived in two opposite worlds; the city and the country. Their world felt foreign to me; upscale and privileged. I enjoyed it but I didn't covet it.

This particular visit was populated with all the other cousins

31

present as well. They were KayKay's cousins on her mother's side so they actually weren't my cousins, and didn't really feel like my family, but we all pretended they were. She lived in a big house with a white picket fence around it; a yard and trees and grass and you could walk out her front door and it was like living in a park!

On this trip, I was finally old enough to hang with the cousins unsupervised. I could kind of take care of myself but they would keep an eye on me as well. I was 4. We, the kids, were all going on an adventure together and I was all in. I had no clue what was up but I was in. We were all going outside to ride bikes around the neighborhood! KayKay had multiple bikes and tricycles that she outgrew but kept for occasions just like this. Very exciting – very "I have no clue what I'm doing – but I'M ALL IN."

Some of the kids brought their vehicles with them from Brooklyn and Queens because when you lived in the city your prized ride was a scooter - the kind made with a wooden milk crate nailed to a 2 by 4 slab of wood with old roller skate wheels attached to it and some cross bar dowel or metal rod as the steering device. It was actually the 'hanging on' device as this only steered forward.

The brakes were your other foot - and depending on your favoring left or right, one of your shoe soles was ground down more than the other. These scooters were geared for sidewalks, not dirt country roads, so they had a tricky time negotiating the rocks and gravel but everyone had a ride and everyone had fun.

This looked like a scene from Junior Japanese West Side Story as a gang of half pints, the oldest being 9, rode all the way down the street and back! There were no cars to worry about as this was Jersey country life in the '50s.

After about 5 or 6 trips, we were sweaty and dusty and we all decided to race back to the house. I was on a tricycle holding my own - always last but still having a blast.

Then it happened. I suddenly felt my panties full - and heavy - and I immediately jumped off the tricycle seat.

The kids yelled "c'mon, hurry up!" and without missing a beat I said, "Ok, I'm just gonna walk back."

I had my cousin's sunglasses on - oversized for me since she was a year and a half older. I pushed them up against my face looking like Audrey Hepburn, tipped my head back a bit to keep them on...and started walking the tricycle back up the street. Slowly. Deliberately. Making sure I looked normal and didn't drop anything on the way.

It felt like a looong journey back and the kids had already put their vehicles away and washed their hands by the time I arrived. I walked into the living room where the mothers were gathered on one side chatting and laughing. I quietly walked up to my mother and whispered in her ear, "I made unko in my pants." She stopped and said, "What?"
So, I whispered again but didn't finish my sentence because that "What?" wasn't because she didn't hear me the first time.
Then she announced to everyone, "Oh my goodness! Louise made unko in her pants!!"

I still remember that recoiling feeling in my stomach that I didn't realize then, was the worst sensation a human could feel. This sensation is the kind of weapon that people employ against one another throughout history. The feeling that you never want to feel that can cause every reaction from battle to suicide.

It was similar to the feeling I had when Rosie bit my finger. I didn't know it was Shame. Embarrassment. Humiliation. Which resulted in Anger. Rage. Revenge. I had no words to identify the feeling but it was way too familiar and way too distinct.

Suddenly I was the center of attention at a time when I wanted to be invisible. I was mortified. Here I was trying to be stealth and cool. This woman blew my cover completely. I couldn't believe she did that. I hated her for what she did. I felt betrayed.

At that moment, I thought to myself, "I will never trust this woman again."

And I didn't.

# 6. LIKE MOTHER...

We didn't have too many more of those situations of betrayal because I didn't let it happen. It was a great lesson for me to learn at 4-years-old, to assess a situation and make a decision to turn everything around if necessary. I knew there was a way I could control things in my world so I could avoid having that feeling again. I learned the concept of trust before I even knew the word. And I knew what it felt like to be the victim of betrayal.

That feeling was worse than falling down and scraping my knees...which I did regularly. But that inner pain was too deep and lethal and I would avoid it at all cost.

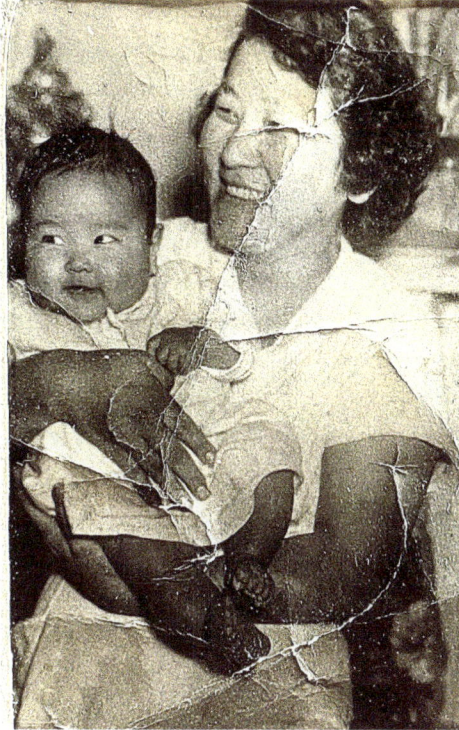

Kimiye "Kay" Mita: age 33 & Moi

The interesting thing I realized was that it was under my control. I actually caused it. I put myself in that situation then I allowed myself to feel it. Yes, I made a mistake - I made unko in my pants. I owned it. But the bigger mistake - I told someone.

Someone I trusted though often questioned. But you're not supposed to question her. She's your mother. You're OF her. Trust isn't even a thing...not yet anyway. I don't have a concept of 'trust' because I'm 4. I just feel things. I don't even know what I feel. I just know what I don't want to feel. Anything associated with that feeling is OUT. Now she was OUT.

Somehow, I was at peace with this knowing. I felt a sense of reserve with her from that point on.

She wasn't the enemy. But she wasn't the ally. I watched what I said knowing she didn't really understand - not like my dad. I could tell him anything. We knew we couldn't tell mom everything and we kept secrets. That began the building of a virtual wall between me and my mom.

She knew my bond with my dad excluded her and I became the other woman. None of this was evident cerebrally; but you could feel it like a chilly wind sweeping across the room when those sensations engulfed her.

Of course, I didn't care because my daddy was MY daddy. And I was definitely the favored child...oh and the only child...who was born when mom was a 33-year-old virgin and dad was 45; oats sewn and time to settle down.

I remember how I felt when she told me that they were older parents, (for that era - the 1950's) and all they wanted was a son. "That is all your daddy and I hoped for; someone to carry on the family name and to be a pillar of a man like his father. But... we had... you."

I think the conversation ended there because I don't recall follow up comments of rejoicing on their part or any warm acceptance of the consolation prize.

That was my first experience of "...AND...?" Crickets. Sealed in stone.

It was the same feeling I had once before when I put my penny in a gum-ball machine and nothing came out.

I never associated disappointment with sadness. That is something one learns; as in all our behavioral responses. My normal response to disappointment was indifference; the shrug that the 2Me's did. …Whatever.

She inevitably bestowed the greatest gifts upon me throughout my early life as her truthful blurts shaped my personality, attitude and temperament. I actually tried to be boyish; a bit tough; physically strong; aloof instead of whiney. I rarely cried. My father once said, "Japanese don't cry." Uh...ok. Wait till they find out I'm not Japanese…

I tried to be the boy they wanted. But…they had…me.

And to top it off when I was being tom-boyish they wanted me to act like a lady... go figure...

I have finally come to realize those were my innate qualities from the beginning. The rough and awkward, goofy and clumsy; a little cold – not sentimental. Calculating self-preservationist. Were those my endeavors to be boyish or was that just naturally me? …Whatever.

If it wasn't for the huge difference between me and my mother I would never be as strong and independent as I was; as I am. If it were not for the great disappointment I was to her, and she to me, I could have followed in her footsteps and decided that she could call the shots and I'd be happy to go along cuz she's my mommy and I love her.

But our polar opposite personalities allowed me to figure out an alternate journey to some degree; as in 180. I wasn't going with the program and falling in line as was expected of me and all kids of that era. "Children should be seen and not heard" was the classic adage that we grew up with in the 50's and 60's. Obedient children were expected and talking back unheard of.

And then there was me. So, my wanting her to understand and be my ally wasn't happening. My behaving and falling in line with status quo was impossible. In the end, we were exactly alike with the exact same dilemma.

I wanted her to understand me and be different from whom she was.

She wanted me to understand her and be different from whom I was. We were twins.

I never realized this until she was gone.

And I could finally love her ... unconditionally.

## 7. THE PICTURE BRIDE

Her mom was a picture bride from Japan who was forced to leave her true love to fulfill the request of my grandfather, a complete stranger, living in Hawaii. His offering to her was a life in the new world and a ransom to her parents and family.

A "picture bride" is one whose photograph is submitted to an agent who then sends it to prospective husbands living abroad requesting a spouse. The prospective husband, in turn, sends his photograph to the agent for viewing by the picture bride along with a substantial offering as a gift for her hand. The agent was basically a legalized pimp.

In this particular situation, the photograph of my grandfather wasn't actually his. It was of a handsome man a decade his junior. Although as deeply heartbroken as my grandmother was, having to leave her true love of choice to honor her parents' negotiation, the photograph provided a consolation to look forward to. New life in the new world with a new very handsome young man; perhaps it's not all that bad.

The month-long boat ride from Japan to Honolulu was met with anticipation on both sides. My grandfather was ready to receive the most valuable purchase of his life thus far, and plant family roots in Hawaii. My grandmother was about to meet her new prince charming and yes, plant family roots in Hawaii too. How proud her parents were and elated for everyone's good fortune!

The boat docked; the plank lowered; the crowd of anxious foreigners filed off in orderly fashion met by officials with immigration paperwork. Time moved in slow motion as they wrestled with language - verbal and written - all dependent upon a handful of translators.

Finally, the arrivers with suitcase in one hand and photograph in the other walked into a sea of receivers with a lei in one hand and photograph in the other, as the game of "match" ensued.

My grandfather had no problem finding his match. My grandmother on the other hand was searching and craning her 4'10" eager self to find the match to her photograph...that didn't exist.

When he found her, my grandfather was more than overjoyed! She was young and beautiful and petite, as good Japanese women were. He rushed up to her and eagerly introduced himself as he claimed his prize without reservation.

She, on the other hand was taken aback by this 6-foot-tall, larger than most Japanese men, older stranger trying to portray the person she was going to spend the rest of her life with - though clearly was not the man in her photograph.

She resisted; he insisted; again, and again; back and forth until emotions were rising on both sides. Finally written paperwork was produced and the charade was uncovered. She was with an imposter. A demanding deceitful being who got what he wanted most of the time - because of his commanding presence. She resigned to her fate, as there was no other alternative.

She married my grandfather and like a true Japanese, held her grudge against him till the day of his funeral.

A year after their marriage my grandmother was able to procure the perfect act of revenge. She gave my grandfather his first child; a girl.

Yoshitaro & Ninoye Tanaka

My mom was the first born of four children. At this writing (ONLY NOW) I realize that she probably experienced the same gum-ball machine reaction upon her arrival as I did.

Three brothers later she was the seasoned nanny responsible for their well-being as all older sisters fatefully were and still are.

My mom would complain that her mom wanted her to dress feminine and be oshare - the Japanese equivalent of wearing make-up, self-grooming and looking like a lady. She was a rugged little tom-boy carting around 3 brothers and making sure their masculine superiority was nurtured every step of the way. No matter what she did, she felt criticized by my grandmother; a constant disappointment and never appreciated.

George 12,  Mike 14,      Dad,   Allen 15,  Mom,  Kimiye 16

All three brothers were taller than average and at full adult height, grew to more than 6 feet tall. She was always tiny, like her mother, and at full womanhood was 5'1.

She recalls taking all three brothers to a movie and carrying the youngest one, George, on her back with his feet dragging on the ground, trying to sneak him in without paying for him, pretending he was a little toddler. She always carried that chip on her shoulder of trying to prove her worth and value...a highly contagious gene that can dangerously be inherited.

If only she realized she and her mother were also twins.
The Gum Ball Machine sentiment was founded by my grandmother, to my knowledge. And buried itself deep in the XX chromosomes of her DNA. It is a miasma that has passed down through the generations.

And frickin' stopped here...I hope...

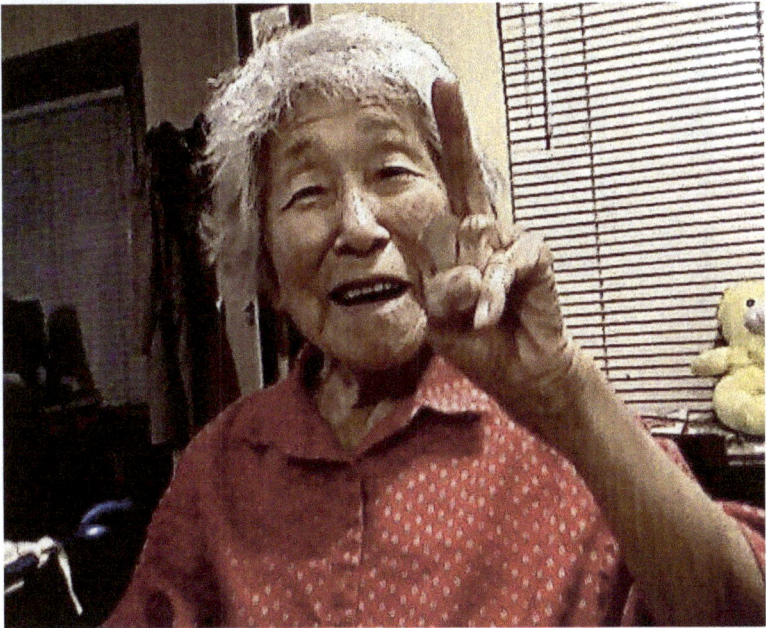

Kimiye Mita age 90

"You're number ONE!"

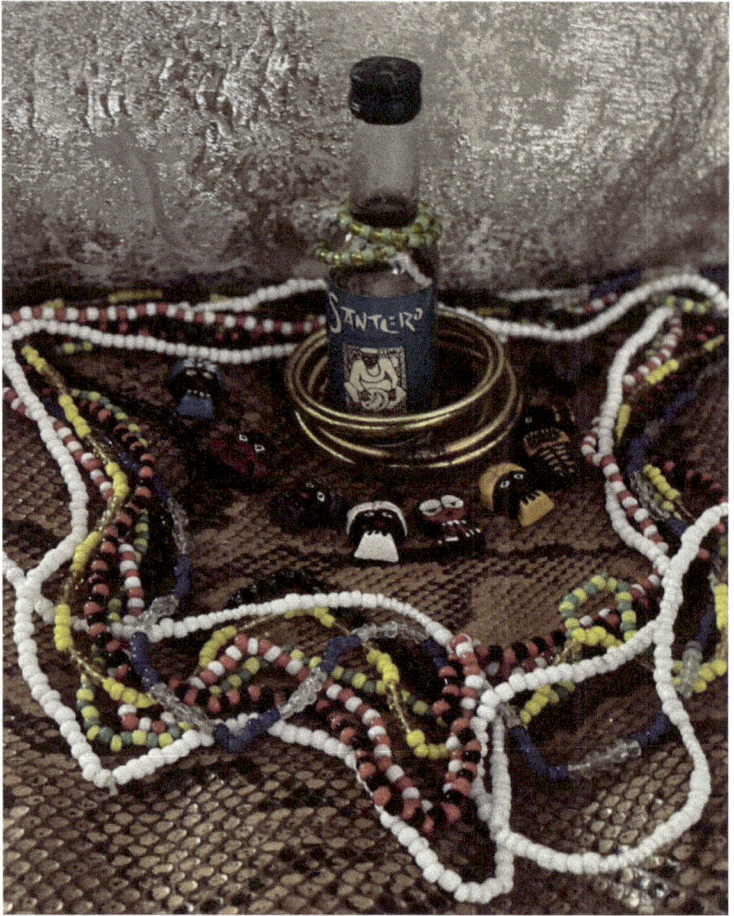

## 8. MANNY

Manny was an anomaly. Everyone knew about him. Well, if you were Latino you certainly knew. He had a place on the ground floor of a building across the street and down the block from my building in the projects. All my neighbors talked about him and how he could heal anybody of anything. When they shared stories their eyes were bugged out and they spoke in loud whispers as if it were a secret they couldn't keep - and the electricity from their excitement made everyone lean in even if they didn't understand Spanish.

He would hold court once a week and that hall was packed to the max. Every folding chair on both sides was occupied; row after row, and unlike church, people clamored to sit closest to the front - as near to Manny as they could be.

His alter was laden with statues and pictures of brown complexioned santos y santas, some bare chested, some wearing bright colorful robes and head dresses.

There were candles and more candles and a golden statue of maybe Jesus draped with fabric and beads. Fruits, rocks, crystals, caracoles, branches of plants and flowers were laid at their feet. Mini shot glasses were filled with wine that he would pour just before the people would enter.

I knew this because I was one of Manny's "assistants." Me and Ernie, the negrito, about a year older than I, were the chosen ones; Manny's helpers.

One day me and Ernie were hanging out down the street in the candy/liquor/grocery store when Manny walked in to get his daily Gypsy Rose and Camels. We weren't afraid of him like most kids and we didn't stare - like most everyone else who didn't know him.

He had shoulder length pressed hair; hot ironed to make it straight and turned under like a page boy - a cross between James Brown and Prince. He wore purple. And black. But mostly purple. He nodded at us. We nodded at him. Then as he walked outside he tipped his head signaling us to follow him.

When we were outside the store he said,

"Ju juanna be my jelpers?"

We looked at each other and semi-shrugged one shoulder and said "uh, sure." He proposed we go across the street with him to his place and he would explain. Being seven I wasn't allowed to cross the street alone but Ernie was eight and he could, so I felt that was supervision enough, under the circumstances.

This was the first time either of us saw the inside of Manny's ... church. We were gobstruck - and not - at the same time. Because as kids everything is new and we never know what is OMG or what is regular. So, we both acted nonchalant - and that made Manny comfortable.

He proposed we come to help him once a week by lining up the chairs nicely, getting him his Gypsy Rose and Camels on that day and mind the collection dish making sure everyone put something in it as they exited the hall after the meetings.

Sounded easy enough and we were hired.

On game day, he was dressed in a long purple velvet cape (looking even more like Prince, though this was 1957 pre-Prince, and the now, late Prince was born in 1958,) with white beaded necklaces layered 10 plus deep over the cape. He would prepare the glasses with the Gypsy Rose; a shot for the gods and a shot for him. He would then go "back stage" until it was time.

Upon Manny's cue me and Ernie opened the doors and greeted the people who poured in limping with canes and crutches, bent over moaning and groaning in agonizing pain. When the hall was filled Manny would make his grand entrance and the audience would bellow a wail of welcome and adoration to begin the ceremony.

Manny settled the audience with an opening salutation and blessing to bowed heads and sounds of weeping. Then with a scrutinizing eye he would select one person who looked the worst in the crowd, to bring to the front, by the alter. He would then tell him or her,

"Juu go to the wessside jaiway and count 100 Cadelacks and when juu get to 100 - juu will be jealed!".

They would go to the back of the hall and exit. Apparently, they would do what he said and yes, they were jealed.

Then the remaining parishioners would come up for his or her blessing. For each individual, Manny, in a voice, sounding like he was in an echo chamber, would chant incantations in notSpanishnotEnglishnotanythingIeverheardbefore.   But they would be invigorated by his words, his gestures, the excitement he invoked! It was pure magic.

Manny's collection dishes were overflowing and it was a good thing there were two of us to handle his wealth. He would give each of us 25 cents at the end of the evening. And another 10 cents each to go fetch his wine and cigarettes. We were making the big bucks baby!!!!

This went on for ages - maybe a month - I felt I had a full-time job that nobody knew about. My mother had no idea where I was for an hour once a week. She thought I was jumping rope on the side of the building out of view from our window.
Don't ask. Don't tell.

Then one day...

We were set up and ready for the crowd that was already waiting outside. Manny was still backstage. We were waiting...and waiting...then we noticed the gods didn't have their offerings. The alter glasses were empty. We went backstage and Manny was laying on the floor...his Gypsy Rose bottle empty by his side.

"Manny...Manny get up...we have to let them in..."

As he struggled to his feet he said "Chure, chure... let them in..."

So we did. They came in with more vigor and need than usual, clamoring for the front seats anticipating Manny's benevolence more than ever.

No Manny. So Ernie minded the crowd smiling and telling them

Manny will be right out in a moment as I went backstage to retrieve him.

He was back on the floor snoring at this point - so I tugged at his cape and tried pulling him up and quietly yelled at him

"Manny you're gonna blow this! They're out there waiting for you!".

"Jokay, Jokay, Jokay I'n coming!!".

Manny staggered out into the hall. The room fell silent. They had never seen him like this. Suddenly he lifted his arms waving them to the sky - looked up and screeched

"LOS DIOS ESTAN AQUI!!!"

and collapsed into a heap on the ground. The entire congregation jumped to their feet screaming,

"GRACIAS A DIOS! GRACIAS MANNY! GRACIAS!!"

...over and over as they wept and bawled, abandoning their canes and crutches and throwing money toward Manny lying on the floor! They were all ecstatic just short of hysteria for they had experienced the ultimate miracle; God entered Manny's body right before their eyes!!

As Ernie and I ushered them out, each person thanking us and blessing us for our contribution to this day, it hit me like an arrow in the forehead: "Manny doesn't heal people. People heal themselves."

49

I had found the holy grail.

## 9. THE CHARADE

My career as an usher came to an end. I returned to being the no income earning seven-and-a-half-year-old with mom & dad being none the wiser for my escapades. I didn't save my money; I managed to consume the entirety in forbidden candy upon every payday with no evidence left to incriminate me or cause suspicion.

Second grade and seven-years-old came to an end. We all retired for the summer to resume in the fall, picking up where we left off but in a new classroom with a new teacher. All the same kids reuniting each year; a half inch taller; a little browner from summertime in New York, playing in the gutter with the fire hydrant opened full blast creating a river of relief from the sweltering heat. We had a resilient immunity that was skillfully nurtured in the hood.

September rolled around and what would be normal wasn't. My destiny took a left turn; something weird happened and suddenly I was headed for fourth grade. Wait…What? Is this some mistake? Huh? Nobody asked me if I wanted to do this. And how did this happen? Uh, what does this mean?

Thus, began the charade.

How does an eight-year-old blend in with nine-year-olds and feel normal? She doesn't.

I don't even know how to be normal as an eight-year-old? I've never done that before either. The leap is huge at that age!

Oh, sure when you're twenty nine and your friends are thirty it ain't no big deal. But at eight with nine-year-olds...huge.

How do I look at everything now?
What do they think is funny?
What do I think is funny?
What do they think is cool?
What do I think is cool?
What do they think is stupid?
What do I think is stupid?
What do they find important?
What do they find boring?

I didn't even consciously think any of those things; it was a blur of "I know nothing" from one day to the next...all the while pretending I did.

If I was short and at the front of the line in second grade, this sealed the deal permanently.
I couldn't even fake it if I wanted to.
I was trying to be more than I was... whatever that meant. And trying not to feel like I'm not enough...whatever that meant too.

We have choice; either it's a ballet or a hockey match. You choose. At least choose to be all in. And I did.

I observed everything everyone did. Who was comfortable in their own skin; who wasn't. Who looked like they were having fun; who looked miserable. Who made it all look easy; who looked like they were struggling. Who looked scared, worried, nervous...and who didn't. I felt like a spy. Or the spook who sat by the door. Paying attention to it all while pretending I was part of it. Little did they know I was trying on personalities to see which one fit; which I could pull off and which yielded the best results. It was what kids do, I suppose, as they figure out who they are. Does everyone see through this masquerade or are we all too busy stumbling over our own costumes to notice the other guys?

The one saving grace about being a kid is we're all too naive to know we're naive.

The way I thought then, assessing, comparing, deciding which direction to go, is the same process of thinking I still employ. I don't discuss it with anyone. I don't want someone else's opinion. I don't want to have to justify mine. It's all by feel. What feels like a good fit. For me. Period.

I see my peers still trying to figure out what fits them best. They are running around naked and don't realize we can all tell when they're cold. But that's another subject altogether.

It fascinates me that my thought process is still exactly the same. My radar of sincerity is always on. My moral compass is always pointing North and those two factors determine if a conversation is worth the air it consumes. It basically comes down to keeping it real.

We all try not to be judgmental but that is impossible. How else would you filter your friendship zone from your no-fly zone? Call it assessment; evaluation; analysis; whatever you want to call it is fine if that takes the prejudice out of it. In the end, it's judgment that draws the conclusion to keep it or throw it away.

Every action requires judgment:

Do I turn the wheel hard or gently?
Do I eat the green part or not?
Do I paddle for the wave now or wait?
Do I say yes or no to the invitation?
Do I wear red or blue?

Each judgment we make comes from experience, knowledge, contemplation and decisiveness happening all at once and often in a split second. Then instinct and reflex cradles that judgment to yield a result we didn't necessarily predict. In the end, the decision made comes from the sum total of all aspects of judgment.

This may even require you to betray your truth in the name of good judgment.

There's a knock at my door.
"We're here to kill all Japanese people. What is your name?"
"Mary Chang." I answer.

That is a judgment call that required no judgment at all.
Our tape measure is long and wide and used as needed when needed.

We've given the concept of 'judgment' a negative connotation as if we should go through life with blinders on, babbling our truths uncensored.

Let's stop pretending we're not judgmental - instead let's not let hate be the basis of our judgement.

*WHEN I WAS A KID*

*When I was a kid I was always small*
*Everybody else looked ten feet tall*
*Everybody treated me like a wimp*
*They said, "You can't hang; you're just a shrimp!"*

*So I'd crawl back in my shell*
*And like a turtle there I'd dwell*
*Lay real quiet; be real still.*
*Give me time to think and chill.*

*Well I had time to find a goal*
*To make a plan and take control*
*To do the things to get me there*
*And, check it out - I was aware*

*To do what's right like I believe*
*And find out what I could achieve*
*I'll come back out when I'm ready*
*A turtle's slow but he sure is steady.*

*Like the turtle and the rabbit running the race*
*Each one moving at his own pace*
*When the rabbit was sure the turtle would lose*
*He kicked back and took a snooze.*

*When he awoke; what a joke.*
*Guess who won – the ol' slow poke!*
*And the moral to this song and dance –*
*Everybody's got a chance!*

*You've got to*
*Trust!*
*I believe in me*
*Trust!*
*I can be who I want to be*
*Trust!*
*Do you believe in you?*
*Trust!*
*Y'know it's what you gotta do!*

(*Exerpt from "Let It Rip," my one-woman show written 30 years later.)

## 10. SYLVESTER

Mom's way of protecting me was via fear. If I functioned from fear I wouldn't attempt anything that could endanger me. She practiced that religion so fervently until she believed it. And lived her life from that pulpit until the end. She reminded me that "You are the smallest, the shortest, the youngest, the poorest, the slowest, the weakest, and by the way don't forget you are a girl and not white..." It couldn't get worse than that...basically the runt of the litter; a litter of one. I was an endangered specie.

The thing is, when you're the smallest it's common to have a chip on your shoulder; a Napoleon complex, as they call it. You try to make up for your shortcomings, (pun totally intended,) and you create an attitude and posture to keep people at bay – backing them off with the notion that you could be dangerous - by shredding their ankles. It's like small dogs; they are yappy and hostile and calling everyone out, gnarling and growling showing their teeth and snapping at you to let you know who's boss. Of course when you approach them unaffected by their threats, they turn and walk away.

Her dogmatic ways (second pun totally intended) contributed to my chihuahuaness out of rebellion and defiance. But I didn't always have that attitude.

Prior to becoming the feisty chihuahua I was cautiously scared most of the time. Staying safe at home in the miserable pits of fear was worse than escape into the unknown dangers of the outside world. So, I had to go. And true there was danger out there.

That's because my neighborhood was ruled by gangs; boy gangs and girl gangs. There were basically 3 gangs who hung together - not with each other – among themselves - and threw attitude at anyone and everyone outside of their gang - their tribal exclusive circle of friends.

I was outside of all circles in every possible way.

The girl gangs would intimidate girls; the boys harassed boys.

The black girls, (known at that time as "colored" girls, which was less offensive than Negro girls and sounded cooler,) was comprised of all shades of cocoa from the African American community, splattered with an occasional Haitian and Jamaican and a real African.

The Spanish gang (pre-'Latina' or 'Hispanic') included Puerto Ricans, Cubans, Dominicans (from the Dominican Republic - DRs as they were known) and Colombians. Surprisingly no Mexicans were living in Harlem and at the time they were considered exotic.

Lastly was the Irish gang - made up of tough Irish Mick-kids from the ghetto. Our ghetto.

This was the beauty of Harlem in the '50's and '60's - an amalgamation of every color in the crayola box and then some. Of course there was the odd Chinese family who ran the laundry and the Chinese restaurant, and us, the Japanese family who was nice and friendly and had a mother from Hawaii, wherever that was. Hawaii and Mexico were exotic lands far and foreign to New Yorkers in Harlem.

These girls had established territorial rights - all to the same location...um - HERE. In other words, if they were hanging out HERE first, you couldn't. They would wolf you if you were alone, so you would make sure never to get caught alone. The threat was real and you'd be scared of the possibility that you would get your ass kicked cuz this was their territory and you better get out of HERE. They made it perfectly clear and everyone knew it.

They never got into actual confrontations with each other, though they would threaten to have a West Side Story scene but they were so young they were just as scared.

When I would go out to play I felt like Tweety Bird avoiding Sylvester the Cat. I'd check out the area and sneak behind a wall or park bench until the coast was clear. If I'd see any girls from the three gangs, I knew that I had to wait till they left before making my break. This went on for years...maybe 2 at the most, but back then that was yeeeaaarrs.

Then one day...

## 11. LULU

I was about nine years old and jumping rope on the side of my building by myself and Lulu and her mother were walking up the street toward me, coming from the grocery store. Lulu was a head taller and twice my body width, though close in age. Lulu's mother, twice as big as Lulu, had a huge blonde beehive and giant red lips making her appear larger than life.

She walked straight up to me forcing me to stop jumping rope. Aggressively she leaned over staring down and confronting me declaring,

"LULU SAID YOU USED THE "F" WORD TO HER!"

She caught me totally off guard as I neither played with Lulu nor ever heard her mother spew anything through those giant red lips.

I stuttered back - "I n-n-never said…" at which point Lulu false cracked me from the side – landing a solid one right on my jaw.

The world stopped. As my head ricocheted back from the punch I automatically went straight for Lulu. I don't recall taking my eyes off of Lulu's mother's face as I grabbed Lulu by the back of her hair with one hand and hauled off upper cuts to her face with the other hand to the rhythm of each syllable proclaiming my innocence.

"I-did-not-say-the-"F"-word-be-cause-I-am-not-al-lowed-to-say-the-'F"-word.

I had never done anything like this before and I have no idea where this came from. It was spontaneous and executed with precision and deliberate accuracy. Must be past life instincts.

Her mother was screaming trying to get me to stop but I was locked on like a pitbull, determined to declare my truth and didn't let go of her until I said my piece. Lulu's face was covered with blood - all coming from her nose – but smearing across her face, giving the impression she was cut everywhere.

A crowd had gathered quickly comprised of representatives from all the nations, genders, age groups and of course, the three notorious girl gangs. Whenever fights broke out it was exciting and we would egg on the fighters regardless of who we rooted for. We just wanted it to last long enough to talk about it for a few days. This one was no exception. Except the odds were exceptional. And the best part was that so many witnessed me being false cracked while her mother distracted me with a phony accusation. There were a lot of hoots and hollers and "whoaaa's' and "daaayam's" and people covering their mouths holding back the "ooh shits" everywhere.

When I broke from my trance I immediately looked for my rope, regaining my composure. It was my prized possession so of course it would not go unattended even in the midst of dire straits. I retrieved it. Then I looked up at my apartment window to see if my mother was watching but I was just out of her angle of sight from the 11th floor. I walked away quickly and into my building before the crowd dispersed. The elevator was waiting as I walked in the lobby and I ran inside and pressed 11 - about eleven times. The adrenaline was melting away as I got to my floor and I walked out of the elevator and down the hall trying to compose myself.

When I got inside the apartment my mother asked, "What was going on down there?"

I gulped; "Did you see…?"

"Yes I did," she interrupted me, "I saw the big crowd. Was there a fight? Were you in that crowd? I was worried for a minute. They looked very excited."

Wait. Really? She didn't know it was me?

"Yeah that's why I came home right away. Too many people. Way too much excitement."

I spent the night praying Lulu's mother wouldn't come knocking on my door to tell my parents that I beat up her kid. Her very big, bigger than me kid.

She didn't.

## 12. THE MORNING AFTER

The drain of post adrenaline rush left me feeling like I had been in 12 rounds with Cassius Clay. At the same time, I discovered a technique that would serve me for the rest of my life. I found that holding my breath was a way to prevent my heart from jumping out of my throat. And it worked. Since then I've used it whenever I was in a pinch. I could arrest fear, panic, sadness, trauma, worry, even being over excited in a good way. I was able to reset to factory settings…before computers did it.

I wasn't nervous enough or resentful enough toward Lulu and her mom to tell my mother the truth; that was not an option. She would undoubtedly put me on permanent house arrest for my own safety. So, I played it off like nothing ever happened.

The only evidence of that day was my freedom from Sylvester. I could walk out of my building anytime I wanted - no matter which gang was occupying the area. I found it interesting that every girl from all three gangs suddenly wanted me to be their friend; "Hey girl! come jump rope with us." "Hey wanna walk to the park & hangout with us?" "You should come be with us."

I know it wasn't my beaming personality that won them over. Were they genuinely impressed or did they think I was nuts and the smart thing to do is make friends with the crazy Chinese girl before she goes postal on them too?

In those days, anyone of Asian descent was assumed Chinese. So, I worked that piece of crazy from that angle too. If someone called out "Hey Chinita..." I'd yell back, "F... you! Soy Japonesa! And don't you forget it!"

I grew up literally next door to a 16 piece Latin band. Tito and Ricardo Marrero's band. They practiced every day, all hours of the day. We lived with the sounds of Tito Puente, Celia Cruz, Eddie Palmieri, Mongo Santamaria. There were trumpets, trombones, saxophones, congas, timbales, vibraphones, pianos, guitar, bass, full set of traps, and percussion for the needy. No one ever complained. There was no on to complain to.

We loved it! Well, my mother and I did. My father would grumble, "Yakamashi! Yakamashi!" It was just noise to him. Meanwhile my mother and I would be moving our feet and hips to the ritmo sabroso!

I loved going next door to hang out and listen to the band. Hah! As if I couldn't hear them through our paper-thin project walls. But it was more fun being there and seeing the band play live.

Gloria, the older sister, taught me how to salsa from the time I was young and I loved it. Sylvia and Jaqueline who lived on the other side of the band would come over as well and it always felt like there was a party going on. This was my music. My roots. To this day if I hear Latin music I have to get up and dance.

If any of the girl gangs was enticing it was the Latina gang. I wanted to be part of them. And Latino boys were so cute. All of them. I even learned to speak Spanish so I would know what they were saying and if they were talking about me.

Pero...

*I saw my friends on the corner one day*
*As I walked up I heard them say,*

*"Thanks for having us over last night.*
*The food, the movie, it was outta sight."*

*Here I thought I was part of the gang*
*I was home alone, my phone never rang.*
*They turned around and they all felt bad.*
*By the look on my face they knew I was mad.*

*Sentia furiosa!*
*No sabia que hacer!*
*Queria gritar a estas muchachas!*
*But then I said to them…*

*Lo que necesita realize*
*Aunque hablo Español there's no disguise.*
*Yo soy Luisa. No soy Chola*
*Y' think I can't hang? Then dejame sola.*

*It takes heart and soul to be my amigo*
*A part-time friend no es lo que sigo*
*If sinceridad is too much trabajo*
*All I can say is "Vete pa'l carajo."*

(\*Exerpt from "Let it Rip")

In the end, my conclusion was ... go solo.
Be everyone's acquaintance.
Reveal no secrets.
Don't proclaim allegiance to anyone.
Because then it will alienate the others.
You don't belong to any of the clans anyway.
Just remain the alien.
It's safer.
Smarter.
Easier.
Keep no secrets with anyone so you don't have to worry about them betraying you.
Keep your secrets to yourself...your true ally.
Period.

Remember, mom taught you that when you were 4.

## 13. GERALDINE

**BELIEFS:** We all have belief systems that determine how our lives function. From our appearance to our choice of associates to what we eat, our beliefs serve us positively or negatively, depending upon the situation. (That's my belief, by the way.) We acquire our beliefs from our parents, teachers, mentors, religious leaders, friends, peers, politicians, advertising, media influence, as well as our life experiences. Our beliefs change from time to time as our needs change and as old beliefs no longer serve us. Sometimes we out grow our beliefs gradually; at other times, we drop them like a hot potato.

For example, when I was a teen I thought drinking alcohol was a sign of maturity and sophistication. My parents didn't drink and I couldn't stand the taste of liquor but all my friends were doing it and I had to play along. Drinking was depicted as "cool" by actors on television and in advertisements everywhere. At the end of the day people would celebrate or relax by having a drink; happy hour, cocktails, a highball; "It's Miller time!" The emphasis on drinking liquor being a pleasurable pastime was everywhere! It was the thing to do.

So, I would have some sweet mixed drink to demonstrate my maturity and "need to unwind," like all mature folks need to do. I had fake ID and passed myself off for a few years older than I was. I'm sure people knew I was underage, but they couldn't stop me if I had the ID. It was torture. Not only did I gag from the taste, I didn't enjoy the feeling of getting drunk or the buzz from booze. It made me red-faced and nauseous. But I put up a front and gargled those suckers down until I hit 18 years old.

Thank God I finally reached the legal age of declared adulthood so I no longer had to fake it! Ironically, in celebration, I stopped drinking that day.

I also remember the religious beliefs that I adopted spanning from one end of the globe to the other in search of an affiliation that I could identify with. I was always inspired by the spiritual lift that was collectively projected by the members of a church or temple. The singing, chanting, wailing, droning, gongs, music, or whatever auditory medium was employed, would send my soul soaring. I remember how it first started.

Geraldine B. lived on my floor down the hall. She went to Corpus Christi School and wore a fabulous blue plaid pleated skirt with a white button down short sleeve blouse every day. White anklets and black Mary-Janes completed the outfit, topped with a sweater or coat depending on the time of year and the weather. New York's four seasons offered us a variety of fashion choices and Geraldine was consistently chic for three quarters of the year.

But on Sundays she killed it! She dressed up to the nines with a different dress each week. Her Sunday church shoes were patent leather with a reflection of the sun in every step. I admired her. I envied her.

One day I asked her about her church going on Sundays - and if she could ever bring me. Parents asked parents and next thing you know I was in a new dress with new Sunday church shoes – red ones because they were on sale since no one else would buy them - ten cents to put in the offering dish and a scarf to put on my head when I entered the church. I couldn't believe it...I thought all my dreams had come true.

That very first Sunday was other worldly. I could hear the music playing from that Hammond a block away as my heart pounded in my ears in counter-point to the organ. The first time I walked up the stairs to that church I thought I was going to heaven. The doors opened and the lights came thru the stain glass windows like vapors from the breath of angels.

I think I must have frozen because someone, probably Geraldine, grabbed my hand and led me down the aisle to a seat. I followed her lead as she curtsied on one knee before entering the row. Then careful not to step on the low padded shelf, we side stepped our way to an open seat. I observed that no one used it as a foot rest, though I was tempted to as my feet dangled once I was settled on the wooden bench.

The words were a blur. It sounded like Spanish but not. In my Puerto Rican/Cuban/Dominican neighborhood there was always enough lengua, ritmo y comida sabrosa to reflect all shades of the rainbow. And the Iglesia was filled with all the Latinos and Irish in the hood, a splattering of colored folk …and me.

I found my niche. This place was amazing. I felt so high hearing the singing and unison psalm reading and the priest was godlier than I imagined God to be. There was so much gold and sparkle and candles and stand up, sit down, kneel, stand up again and sit down and open your book and read from exactly this page and this paragraph. Man, they had their program down to a T. What a show!

The basket came around just as Geraldine and my mother told me. Everyone in my row put a clinking contribution to the pile. When it got to me I felt the weight of the immense faith and respect this carried, and as I put my dime in the basket and heard it clink, I could see the shiny coins of love that we all committed. I carefully passed it on to Geraldine - I had found my family.

As time went on I knew all the psalms, the Latin responses to the Priest's incantation. I knew when to stand, to kneel, to sit, without looking to my side for confirmation. And I knew just what to do when my favorite part of the entire service came up: communion. I was holier that holy when we ate Jesus's body and drank his blood. And I loved me some grape juice anyway because we never had it at home.

I remember the first time I took communion the wafer stuck to the roof of my mouth and thought I was going to choke to death or gag and embarrass myself and Geraldine but thank God we got some grape juice to wash it down. I later learned to master the art of keeping it on my tongue until Jesus gave us his blood.

My dad was a practicing Buddhist which meant he prayed to his personal Gohonzon and we went to the Buddhist Academy on Saturday to see Samurai movies, of which Zatoichi was my favorite; The Blind Swordsman.

Zatoichi was chubby, unshaven, yogore and poor, eating his meager bowl of rice when a group of nasty samurai would try to sneak up and ambush him. He'd indicate with a tip of his head that he noticed a fly buzzing nearby and calmly snatch it out of the air with his chopsticks and pop it into his mouth - alerting the samurai that, even with his absence of sight, he was still far more clever than they anticipated.

Then bam! Suddenly the fight would begin! He'd rise up drawing his sword simultaneously slashing two or three guys at once. His minimal moves to their exaggerated clumsy attacks made him my hero. When the last intruder fell to the ground (in true over-the-top Japanese theatrical slow motion) he sat back down and resumed eating his bowl of rice.

Super cool...he was my hero. I was going to grow up to be like Zatoichi... definitely with sight...and hopefully beardless.

My mom was a practicing agnostic with a leaning toward the Presbyterians as they seemed innocuous enough. She never went to church or made mention of God or Buddha. But she was the one who bought me the Sunday church clothing. It may have been her way of investing in case God was real.

I noticed Geraldine would get dressed up for a couple of hours Saturday morning and wondered what that was about. After about a year and a half I enquired and was stunned to find out there was a party I was missing - never even knew about! She confessed about confession. How cool was this?

I was pretty good in general anyway since I started this church thing. After all there was no way I'd have a third pair of shoes, ever, if it wasn't for this. School shoes. Play shoes. That's it. Buy them too big - get blisters because they would rub; grow into them; wear them ragged; get blisters because they were too small; then they'd finally wear out - another reason to thank God; then get a new pair and start all over again.

The play shoes were sneakers that got worn to bits; sometimes sooner than later if the skates dug into the rubber too deeply. We had the metal on metal with metal wheels that clamped on to the edges of the soles of your shoes and fastened with a leather strap across your instep for good measure. Sometimes when you'd skate fast downhill and make a stop by skidding sideways the skates stopped while the shoes kept going and they would lift the bottom of your sneakers off. Bad news.

Anyway, confession seemed like a great business deal! You could be bad all week and on Saturday go tell the priest you were; he'd give you a few rounds of Our Father and Hail Marys and everything was wiped??? Amazing!! I loved the idea! Plus, I loved saying them anyway and I had my own rosaries that Geraldine's mother bought me for Christmas. This whole concept actually opened the door to the possibility of me being naughty...oooooh that definitely had an appeal. After all I was going on twelve. So, I talked it over with Geraldine and we rehearsed for a couple of months. Then I pitched this to my parents who thought it was slightly ridiculous but since I already had the shoes, what the heck.

One fine Saturday Geraldine and I walked up to Corpus Christi Church and all the sinners were sitting and standing in line to be absolved of their wrong doings. I was proudly one of them.

The line moved slowly as we were a rough neighborhood and a lot of sinning was probably the norm. Finally, our turn. Geraldine went in first. In less than five minutes she was liberated and came out looking like a freed convict.

My turn. This was someplace I'd never been before. That mini-telephone booth that looked dark and cramped was slightly intimidating. I had seen it on Sundays but it never occurred to me that one day I would enter and rat on myself ...

I walked it; readjusted my eyes to the dimness; the priest was waiting in the other booth. The window slid back and he appeared top lit looking spooky and ghostly. I said...

"Bless me father for I have sinned. This is my first time in confession. I've been coming to this church every Sunday for two years and I have never missed a day. I take communion and know just what to say and do. I have never been baptized and..."

I didn't have enough time to exhale the last words of my sentence when the priest popped out of his booth like a piece of burnt toast.

"GET OUT! GET OUT OF THIS CHURCH AND DON'T COME BACK UNTIL YOU ARE BAPTIZED!"

I froze...like in a dream when the monster is about to chase you and you turn to run but you can't.

Like a bad internet connection that freezes in the middle of streaming a live sports event.

Like you wish you could just have a heart attack so this shit could be gone and you'd wake up somewhere else wondering if that really happened.

"I SAID GET OUT! GET OUT!"

So I unfroze. And got up feeling like the atmosphere was molasses and the peanut butter on the bottoms of my shoes wouldn't let me go faster.

I wasn't the only frozen being; every sinner in line was frozen with a look of horror on each one's face. They probably thought I confessed to burning down the local orphanage. I tried not to look at them but their faces and expressions are indelibly burned into my memory.

The shock rendered me calm...well numb, actually. Mortified. Devastated, I suppose. I didn't know that word at 12.

I think my heart stopped.

Completely.

I walked home slowly.

Thinking one thought.

GOD IS DEAD.

## 14. THE REVOLUTION

"How did it go?" my mother asked without looking up from her dishes.

"Not good." I muttered.

"Oh really." she responded without further enquiry.

"Not going back to church."

"Oh. Ok." She knew it was something. She knew it would be an awkward conversation. She knew I was pissed. Hurt. Off. Weird. She knew she didn't really want to know. She didn't want to feel uncomfortable. So, she left it alone. Gotta love her for that. She knew me. She knew herself.

And never the twain shall meet.

I put away the church shoes. I put away the church dress. No more church paraphernalia. Rosaries rolled up and stuffed in the back of somewhere so that I would never find them again.
And I didn't.

Blue jeans and a black turtleneck became my uniform. The Village - Greenwich, in case there is question, was alive with change. It was 1962 and the movements – plural - had begun.

What a great time to be in New York. What a great time to be all the things I learned to be ashamed of. Actually, I had been ashamed for not being all the things I wasn't: white, male, rich. So now I could step into accepting who I was - since I really could not change those fundamental aspects of myself. It wasn't so much about being proud of who I was; it was permission to not feel like shit.

The silent minority became the vocal majority as protests and demonstrations gathered hundreds of like-minded spirits ready to stand up for themselves and each other.

Washington Square the home of the revolution.

New York was brimming with pride, participation, purpose, power, and persistence. "We Shall Overcome" was the theme song that inspired our movement...civil rights and rights of civility were the plight.

How is it that we're still fighting for that same thing sixty years later?? I live and breathe these rights every minute of every day.

And I still demonstrate:

*By example shall we teach*
*For words are hollow when we preach.*
*Let our children see the strength*
*It takes to go the extra length.*
                              *...Moi*

I traded the Bible for Lao Tsu's Tao Te Ching, Herman Hesse, Albert Camus, Alan Watts and never looked back.

The road to conformity disappeared – wait; hold on a minute; I wasn't conforming to non-conformity... was I?

It opened up the world of beliefs to the world of the unbelievable.

God Bless the Catholic Church. It changed my life forever!

## 15. C'EST MOI

Everyone doesn't need to know what you're thinking or not thinking. Actually no one really cares either. We're all busy figuring out what the hell is going on in our own little world so your situ is not at all my priority, let alone even on my list.

There is so much you want to say but knowing it is futile you can spare the chin wag and keep those thoughts to yourself. "MYOB" my mother used to say. i say "STFU"

We are each doing the same thing - trying not to drown in our mind chatter. Sometimes it comes like a flood and keeping our head above the cacophony of what if's, shoulda, coulda woulda,...is about all we can handle in one go. Sometimes I need a nap just to get away from myself.

"Back in the day," as we say when we are preparing you for a statement that is either out-dated or just totally different from the beliefs, actions, customs, behavior, etc. of today's society - we didn't air our personal thoughts, feelings and daily activities publicly on platforms available to strangers, let alone to people who might know us; family, friends, colleagues, co-workers. We were private for reasons of discretion, safety, most of all - fear of embarrassing ourselves.

Nowadays we want the world to know what we had for breakfast, how we felt about it and if it benefited our process of elimination... to which others actually respond with "likes' and comments. All this supporting the continuation of said catharsis...today, tomorrow and the following tomorrow. Wow...

In spite of my desire to blend in and be somewhat invisible, that was not going to be possible.

I always stood out. Ironically because I was short - the shortest and smallest in the class - that put me in the front row, and the first person in the front of the line.

Being in the front row forces you to 'bring it' whether you want to or not. Your exposure to the enemy - whether it's the teacher or those greeting the front liners puts you in view - we see you; you're making an impression in my mind. There are two impressions you can make: one, "I'm going to remember you!" or two, "I'm not."

The first, "I'm going to remember you" can be caused by the favorable note you struck; you stood out as interesting. Or you look like trouble and I'm going to etch your face in my mind so I know who to look for when things go south.

The second, "I'm not going to remember you" comes from your benign appearance, uninteresting presence or you look like a non-threatening good guy. I can count on you to not make trouble. So now I can forget about you.

We all make our choices; how we want to be perceived, if at all. Thinking like a ninja, I would opt for the second. Or foreseeing that I might stir up some shit, I would be better off invisible.

I was not an over achiever with my hand raised - "Oh pick me! Pick me!" But I wasn't shy or timid either. Just trying not to make an ass of myself most of the time. And not sure where that quest came from, let alone if I was ever successful.

I suppose everyone's mission as a kid is to be cool. Don't do anything to make a fool of yourself. Don't say the wrong thing; don't wear the wrong shoes; don't wear a blue shirt on red shirt day... do not be the last guy chosen to be on the team...and that mindset follows us throughout the rest of our lives.

We want to be the cool person; the one everyone admires or wants to follow...the one that said the right answer...the one that had a good idea...a clever invention...proclaiming an AHA that made everyone say AHA!! And at the very least - not be the one we roll our eyes at and say (or think) "that was dumb."

In my effort to be cool I was a bit of a bully at times. Bob Dylan used to sit in front of the Café Wha? on Bleeker Street, playing his guitar and … "singing." We all knew him as a fixture on the sidewalk. He had no pitch; but he had no tone either. I'd walk by him and say, "Stop, Bob, you're killin' me. You know you can't sing…just stop!" He'd laugh and keep right on "singing."

Who knew he'd end up becoming… Bob Dylan?

We all wanna be loved…or even just liked.

For most of us...it's a work in progress...to this day.

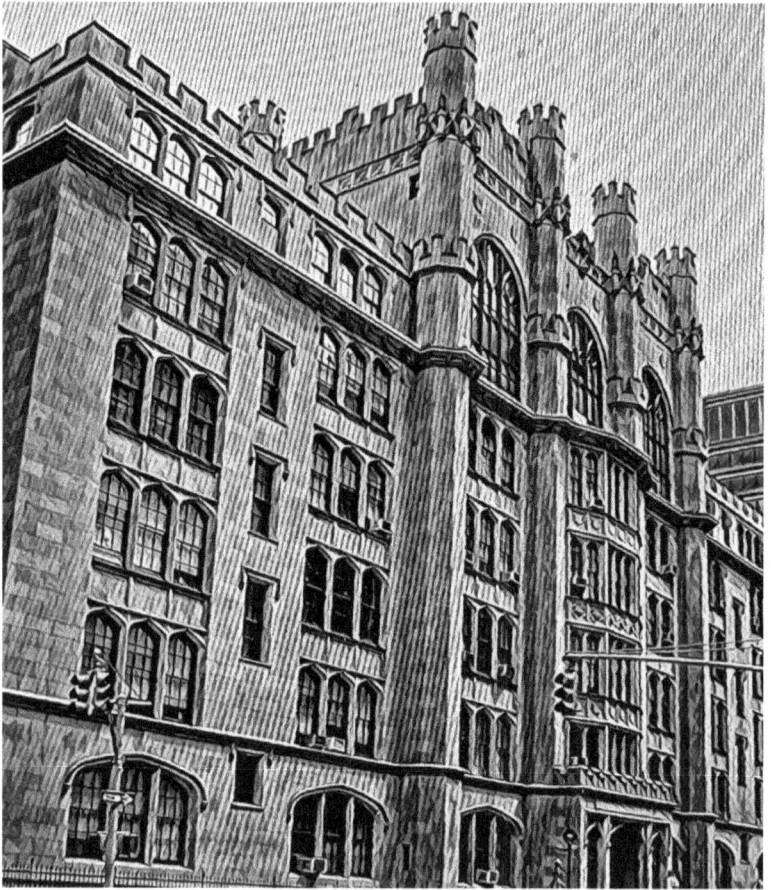

Hunter College High School
68th-69th Street and Lexington Avenue, NYC

## 16. HUNTER

There are times when you feel awkwardly out of place but you manage to blend in thinking no one would notice you're different and you could just piddle along like everything was normal.

This wasn't one of those times.

Somehow in sixth grade I took a test that I didn't know I was taking and, somehow, I passed said test and somehow got admitted to another school on planet Jupiter without my knowledge or consent. The only remotely familiar thing about this situation was that the feeling it invoked was similar to the one I had at the end of second grade.

All the sixth graders of PS 125 were going to PS 43 in September. All the students that took three full years to break in and bond with, and mold into 'friends' were going to PS 43 without me. I was being shipped off to another planet with total strangers in a foreign land - the upper east side of Manhattan.

We lived in a low income housing projects in Harlem. The Grant Projects. A nice housing project - new when we moved there in 1956 so it felt like our home. The neighborhood was my neighborhood. I knew a lot of people - by face - in my neighborhood. They knew me - being the only Japanese family in the projects. they knew me by face too. It wasn't warm and fuzzy but it was familiar - and home.

This new school was 3 subway train rides away. I'd have to leave an hour and a half before school started to get there on time.

This was Hunter. It was a semi-exclusive all-girls school. Hunter's admissions started at kindergarten and continued through college, with entrance exams in sixth and ninth grade and, of course, for freshmen entering college.

They called it an IGC school, (for Intellectually Gifted Children.) Only 6% of the students who take the exam get in; this means that it is harder to get into Hunter College High School than it is to get admitted into Harvard, a school with an 8% admission rate.

All girl classmates for the entire lifetime of your education...if you were considered smart. If I was really smart I would have flunked the test so this option wouldn't upheave my normal life and banish me to Jupiter.

Of course my parents were thrilled for this opportunity and more grateful than proud for the privilege of their ghetto daughter to be allowed to attend such a prestigious school. It must have been a fluke.

If I learned anything from the leap of second to fourth grade it was to be cool. Say nothing. Observe. Assess the situation and figure out how to play this hand so you don't make a fool of yourself.

But this was Jupiter. Nothing like I'd ever experienced before. Even the air was thinner.

This was my first experience of seeing critters of a similar demographic seek each other out and bond instantly. It felt biological; an act of evolution or survival of the misfits.

There was THEM, the entire population of Hunter, and then there was us.

Five girls from ghettos around New York City were admitted to the seventh grade at Hunter...and we found each other. It was organic, magnetic, immediate...it was wonderful and we felt instantly at home with each other. That must be where the expression "homies" comes from - though not in 1961. But we certainly were homies.

There was a tall Russian immigrant, Natasha, who we called Natalie; a skinny Puerto Rican named Mary - whitened from CarmenRosaMariana; a chubby colored girl named Cleo - yes short for Cleopatra, who was clearly no longer Negro, yet gingerly breaking into the moniker "Black" in those days; and a Jewish girl, Hannah, who was a temporary homie but thought better of associating with us and tried to assimilate with THEM. I'm not sure how well she did but she managed to stiff arm us like a running back with the ball in the fourth quarter, within the first month at Hunter.

We knew our common denominator was being poo - that's too poor to afford an 'r.' And it didn't bother us. We goofed on 'THEM' and played off our economic difference as if nobody knew.

The girls at Hunter came from parents who were diplomats, department store owners, professors, doctors, lawyers and Indian chiefs. (yes, one girl's father was the CEO of an East Indian Trading Company.) How would we know this? They all asked each other, "what does your father do?" It was a common question in Hunter - immediately assessing if you were worth associating with. Were you in their same cla$$ category or were you the peasant that you appeared to be?

My father delivered groceries for a Japanese food market. He delivered to the seven Japanese restaurants in New York at that time in a car that belonged to the food market. I actually thought it was pretty cool because occasionally I'd go for a ride in his company car on a delivery. We'd arrive at a restaurant and the waitresses were always happy to see him and offer us tea and a Japanese sweet. It was that same special feeling I remembered from the diner in Harlem. I felt proud being my dad's daughter.

But at Hunter, that wasn't going to cut it.

Along with my three homies I made up a profession of dignity that couldn't be traced or verified.

"I'll tell you if you swear to secrecy. My father is a spy."

And they believed me. Or were too appalled or flabbergasted to say otherwise.

I survived the first two years with flying colors and great grades. Making the trek every morning on three subway rides and bonding with my homies in the hallways and lunchtime when I'd see them.

But I no longer had friends in my neighborhood as they excommunicated me when I got admitted to Hunter. They gave me the cold shoulder as if I thought I was better or smarter; which I clearly didn't and wasn't. But there was nothing I could do about it.

I did have one friend, Roz, who was the only other Japanese girl in our neighborhood. She lived 2 blocks away but we managed to stay friends even though we weren't in the same class at PS 125 and didn't go to the same school after 6th grade. We didn't have the same interests or a whole lot in common other than being Japanese. But we did see eye to eye and had a cold blooded honest relationship. We weren't huggy warm and fuzzy. But we were tight. Super tight. She was my best friend.

I remember we were so close that one day it started snowing and she was at my house. I let her wear my favorite white rubber boots so we could go outside to play in the snow. We got into an argument and she took off the boots and smacked me in the head with them, threw them on the ground and walked home. I stood there stunned, with snow in my face and hair and watched her walk away. I was so pissed off but more stunned by what she did. No one had ever pulled something like that on me! (Everyone knew about Lulu.) I was never going to speak to her again.

That lasted about a week. We've known each other since we were about 5. Holy crap...that's a loooong time. She certainly is my oldest friend, as in, I've known her the longest of any living human on the planet. And she still is my best friend.

*Picture Day:*

*We were both 5 years old.*

*Roz looking neat & poised; Me looking like I fell off the back of a poultry truck.*

That last year at Hunter was torture; I was interested in boys and there weren't any at school. I had no friends besides Roz at home. I lost interest in school work and just was trouble waiting to happen.

I'd sit by the window on the Lexington Avenue side of the classroom. When a young male would walk by I'd yell "A boy!". And all the girls would jump up and run to the window and we'd whistle & cat call him! The teacher would lose control of the class, of course, and I was in the principal's office immediately. This happened about once a week. My parents started visiting Hunter more often than they ever wanted to.

I was grounded till I was 20. Life was a bore.

Then the topper was the shy science teacher, Mr. Brian. He was timid around the students and tried to be scientifically detached but he was cute behind his black rimmed scholarly glasses. He was also youngish for a teacher - mid-twenties tops. He would slouch and try to suppress any manliness from showing but we all giggled around him. Foolishly, he showed his terror... aahhh... we could smell the scent of prey. And I was such a naughty predator. I always smiled at him - not in a sexual way but in a "Oh Mr. Brian you're in trouble" kinda way. And he knew it.

One afternoon my homies and I decided to pull a prank on him. Well, I decided to, and enlisted them as the supporting cast. School was over and the halls were empty. We hid in his office knowing he had to return to get his belongings before going home. He had a wonderful life size skeleton hanging on a stand with wheels that he used for biology class.

We could hear the clicking of his loafers as his footsteps got closer and closer...

Then just before he got to the door I gave the skeleton a shove, rolling it into the hallway! Mr. Brian screamed and threw his books in the air and ran all the way back down the hallway!

We made our break and ran out of his office laughing and making our getaway as quickly as we could, looking back at him, still running down the hall. We laughed and laughed with tears running down our faces for an hour as we debriefed in the local soda fountain!!! This was the highlight of our time at Hunter!!

Well, the next day my mother got the call.

Somehow they knew it was me... Whaaat? I can't imagine how they would assume that????

Two days later we had that meeting with my mother, me and the principal. My father, the spy, was delivering groceries so he was excused.

The principal told my mother that my grades were crap. I wasn't studying. I was causing trouble.

She proceeded to tell her what I did, and how I coerced the other girls to join me. That I often get lots of girls to go along with my mischievous pranks.

"Mrs. Mita, and now your daughter has traumatized the biology teacher."

My mother hung her head halfway down and glared at me sideways, shooting daggers at me, at the same time.

"He'll be in therapy for life."

Then a few more confirming accusations, anecdotes and justifying reasons for her conclusion of the inevitable.

"Mrs. Mita, we're expelling Louise at the end of this semester."


I got kicked out of Hunter.

## 17. LEMONADE STAND

I indeed brought shame upon my parents and had to bear the wrath and guilt of their only child wasting the gift of an opportunity to become something. "I coulda been a contender." But this being the greatest disappointment I could foist on my parents at 14 allowed me so much freedom from worrying about being a screw up in the future.

A career I succeeded in, brilliantly.

I totally understand why some people are under achievers; there are no expectations of them so they can never let you down. How perfect. How not me.

There were so many moments in my life when the worst thing that could possibly happen to me would soon be followed by the best experience ever, which could never have happened without the previous disaster. We've all had that experience. Once. Twice. Nineteen times. Have you made the correlation yet? How long did it take you to connect those dots?

How many times have you pushed the envelope, pushed your limits, pushed your luck, until it ran out? There you are, left with the broken bones, broken promises, broken marriage, broken heart…all preparing you for the biggest epiphany of your life.

The changes you made because there was no other choice, put you in that place of stepping up and bringing something out of you that you didn't know you had. And it happened time and time again.

Right around the corner from the worst catastrophe you could ever experience lies the best thing that could ever happen to you.

It's that old adage, "When you're given lemons make lemonade." I had a lemonade stand.

Things would go south for me often enough that I was almost excited when the shite hit the fan. Oh goodie! What's up next?!! (no, that's not a typo; I hear my Brit friends call it "shite" with a long "i" and it somehow makes "shit" lose its profane nature; making "shit" not so "shitty.")

I recall, as an adult, when my car was stolen and I was talking to the police filing out the report, I could feel myself getting giddy with excitement. The cop immediately became suspicious that I staged the theft and started interrogating me with an aggressive edge.

I of course wanted to enlighten him with my observation of the sequence of life's lessons and my many experiences, but I wisely decided that I should keep that to myself. I gave myself an inner smack and dug up my best distraught-damsel-in-distress performance, but it was like taking a u-turn in an intersection - those don't go unnoticed.

I had forgotten the golden rule:

Silent Thoughts Foster Understanding or **STFU**.

## 18. SILENT THOUGHTS FOSTER UNDERSTANDING

My grandson was about 18 when he shared one of his philosophies of life with me. "When in doubt **STFU**."

It sounds so simple but it is all encompassing.

The brain processes 11 million bits of information per second.

The subconscious mind processes 20 million bits per second.

The conscious mind processes 40 to 50 bits.

The subconscious processes 500,000 times more.

What is the difference between the brain and the mind, you ask?

You can touch the brain.
You can't touch the mind.

(Did you just imitate MC Hammer's "Can't Touch This" and envision him in his low crotch pants doing his sideways crab dance? You even heard the music too? See what I mean about too many thoughts?)

We actually have about 30-40 thoughts that consciously go through our mind per minute.

"Did I lock the door? Do I have my lipstick on properly? Where are my keys? I have to pick up milk on the way home. Who was that woman on the bus staring at me? Did I turn the stove off?" Etc, etc, etc.

There are even some people who are compelled to share their stream of consciousness with any available listener, too!!

(OMG. Don't make eye contact. Keep walking. Look the other way. Do not engage! You could get enlisted, you, the innocent bystander.)

One of the keys to relationships is communication. Some people communicate their thoughts as a monologue. There is no room for response or rebuttal because they really don't care what you think.

Are you listening to what they are saying?

Do you want to cut them off or disqualify them halfway through their speech?

Are you actually listening or just waiting for your opportunity to talk or retort and "listening" is just waiting for the other person to take in oxygen and leave an opening for you to jump in.

At which point your monologue begins.

Even if you disagree with the other person, you don't have to interrupt them and interject your opinion right now. Actually, by you waiting and listening to the entire soliloquy the speaker completes his task and in doing so, leaves nothing left on the table.   Ok, now it's your turn.

Conversations can go back and forth like a tennis match. They don't have to be competitive. They can be engaging, challenging, demanding of your best shot. They can be creative, expansive, provoking, exhilarating and satisfying if you play all out.

Because we don't agree does not justify an argument. Contradiction is stimulating if we can hear each other. It can be educational. That's what we call a debate.   If our focus isn't on being right and making the other guy wrong, we can actually learn something.   If at the very least, different opinions exist...and can co-exist.

Nowadays conversations are a lost art as we're delegated to text messaging and the rhythm of timing and interaction is nil due to the lag between responses. If both are actually texting back and forth because time permits undivided attention to this text-versation, the question in my mind arises:  Why can't we just talk? It would be easier and we could get this over with, faster.

Again, my grandson answers the question I didn't vocalize;

"I text you because I don't want to talk to you."

Thank you.

And thank God my reptilian heritage allows only ice to flow through my veins. No, my feelings aren't hurt by his honesty...honestly.

Texting is an exercise in monologuing.  Even the text messages become abbreviated with short cuts that become a game of "What the heck could that possibly mean?"

It is somewhat entertaining like Mad Libs used to be when you had to fill in the blanks and figure out the complete intended thought. The texter knows what he/she is saying and leaves the mystery up to the textee to figure out.

When the text messages become a barrage of acronyms, and with generational slang and new language being born every day, there is so much room for confusion and faux-pas.

I remember my good friend texting me saying, "Hey I heard your mother died. LOL."

The problem with texting is that more often than not, one is interrupted by something of greater urgency, importance or interest and one party leaves the convo (another abbreviation) unfinished with the last writer hanging - like an unrequited high five.

You say to yourself "...AND?...". Crickets...

My grandson's other philosophy was "Only break one rule at a time," which would have done him well if he adhered to it.

It's not surprising that the advice you give is the advice you need most.

# 19. Y'KNOW...

We live life and do what we do - then make up the reasons for it later. Sometimes much, much later.

What I find so interesting is the feelings I had as far back as I can remember are the same today. The sensation; interpretation; response; thought - even though the verbiage wasn't there at the time - and now, though waxing poetic - it's still the same thought coming from the same feelings. I haven't changed. The essence of me that knows....knew then...and knows now.

How we process our thoughts seems to be innate within and never really changes as we grow up. Intellectually we learn other ways to behave that are more acceptable by the masses; meaning it doesn't make others feel threatened or uncomfortable or having a need to pay attention or be on guard. We establish these rules and abide by them for the majority of our lives until they become the norm.

Many a moment enveloped me in waaaay too much conversation with myself - guiding me down the rabbit hole of confusion and doubt. Thinking and thinking again. Thinking it over and under and looking at all sides. The endless quest of trying to make the right decision. More so, not wanting to make the wrong one. Six one way and half a dozen the other. Do the right thing. For whom? For me? For you? For them?

In the process, we unremember how to know. Or that we even do know. We don't really forget - that would be tragic. But we practice unremembering until it's almost perfected. As life goes on triggers come up that make us remember - even for a brief moment. These moments feel like a relief as we get in touch with reality once again. It's like returning home. Familiar. Easy. Simple. Calming. To know. You just...know.

I think the more educated we become we shape our destiny based on accumulated information. We learn how to make decisions only based on sensible deep contemplation of all the facts and balancing the scales of those facts until one side weighs the winner. We learn to live life in the cerebrum; a small space of cluttered content that goes through processes over and over that render the same outcome; certain uncertainty.

We rely on logic. On deduction. On A plus B equal C. Like balancing your check book. What a sigh of relief when totals match and your calculations are correct. (I've never sighed that sigh. This is speculation based on a metaphor that I don't actually have an experience of, but you probably can relate.)

This way of information based knowledge becomes the norm and although flat in feeling, there is some solace in its safety. It's a formula that the majority adheres to so it's safe to base a life of ignoring the knowing and relying on the knowledge...and being a part of the majority...rather than apart from the majority.

Sounds good on paper. Then a decade goes by. And another. And another. And you suddenly wake up. Something magical happens in your life - a tragedy; a catastrophe; a death; a divorce; and you awaken from the stupor that you've been in forever up to this very moment.

Good Morning… You!!! Good morning ME!!!

It wasn't decades for me. Every year something would happen that reinforced the knowing of the year before. I never understood why my perspective wasn't that logical thinking one of everyone around me. I didn't think like everyone else. It was as if they were growing up and learning how to conform into the beautiful mold and become a vital cog in the machinery of society and I was stuck with that same debate I always had. Is it Thinking? Is it Knowing? Thinking? Knowing?

It felt like trying to jump double dutch and waiting for the right timing of the ropes to jump in and you keep leaning inandoutandinandout - forthandbackandforthandback - until someone yells "c'mon already!" And either your timing is perfect and you kamikaze in there and start dancing away or you tangle the ropes and end up on the outside turning.

Either way I lose. I lose my turn or I lose myself.

Then it dawns on me. I don't have to play this game! I don't jump rope anymore!

Not for them. Not for me! Not for anyone!! I'm done!

Suddenly I feel like I've arrived at a party!

And look - the 2Me's are here!

And I'm so happy to welcome Me to the party!

And look - You're here too!

We're all here at last!

103

The conversation would seem to be foreign but We're fluent in this language. We suddenly feel confident and at ease.

We're speaking the Mother Tongue and it all comes back in an instant.

WELCOME HOME!

I suddenly realize I've come full circle!

Now all I want is more of the KNOWING!

It blows My mind and raises My happy meter a thousand percent.

This is where I want to spend the rest of My life…

Aaahhhh…I see…so do You!!!

And it's easier done than said.

About the Author:


Louise Mita, founder of Integrative Quantum Medicine™ has studied metaphysical alchemy, healing, and martial arts since 1968 and began teaching her trademark philosophies in 1998. Her background includes Parapsychic Sciences, Reiki, Hawaiiana, Kendo, Kung Fu, Aikido, Hapkido, Jeet Kun Do, and Sho Kon Do. Her focus is upon the practical application of these energies to our daily lives as taught in lectures and seminars worldwide.

Louise also had a 40 career as a choreographer and dancer performing in movies, theatre, videos, stage and television. She had her own dance studio, a one woman show, "Let It RIP" and was the founding director and producer of three dance companies, winning over 17 grants and awards, as well as being appointed Dance Commissioner of the Hawaii State Department of Culture and Arts.

Louise was the managing director of the Quincy Jones, "Listen Up" Foundation when they initiated the building of 100 homes in South Africa, as a promise to Nelson Mandela.

She is also a certified practitioner and teacher of Chinese Energetic Medicine, Tai Chi, Qigong, and Feng Shui.


Visit taoenergy.com for more information.

I call this book *"Easier Done Than Said"* because life is... and *"Volume I...in case I decide to write more"* because I have so much more to share in Volumes II, III, etc.

But as Quincy Jones once said to me, "At my age I don't buy green bananas."

So, I thought it wise to get this out to you right now, and if there is more time and an insatiable desire to expound further...I can...and perhaps I will.

Thank you for being a part of Volume I.

www.ingramcontent.com/pod-product-compliance
Lightning Source LLC
Chambersburg PA
CBHW072204090426
42740CB00012B/2385